Mastering TikTok Ads: A
Comprehensive Guide to Advertising Success

Norman A. Wilkins

PUBLIC NOTICE

Table of Contents

Foreword

By following the strategies, tips, and techniques outlined in this ebook, you will be equipped with the knowledge and skills to run effective TikTok ad campaigns that engage your target audience, drive conversions, and maximize your return on investment. Get ready to unlock the full potential of TikTok advertising and take your brand to new heights of success!

Chapter 1: Introduction to TikTok Ads

In this chapter, we will delve into the world of TikTok Ads and explore the immense potential it holds as a marketing platform. We'll uncover the benefits and advantages of advertising on TikTok and introduce you to the various types of TikTok ads available. Let's dive in!

1.1 Understanding the Power of TikTok as a Marketing Platform

TikTok has revolutionized the social media landscape with its unique blend of short-form video content, creative filters, and a massive user base. With over 2 billion downloads worldwide, TikTok has become a global phenomenon, particularly among the younger generation.

As a marketing platform, TikTok offers unparalleled reach and engagement. Users spend hours scrolling through an endless stream of entertaining videos, creating a perfect opportunity for businesses to capture their attention and promote their products or services. TikTok's algorithm is highly effective at showcasing content that aligns with users' interests, making it an ideal platform for brand exposure.

1.2 Benefits and Advantages of Advertising on TikTok

Advertising on TikTok provides numerous benefits and advantages for businesses:

a) Massive User Base: TikTok boasts a vast and diverse user base, with a significant presence across various age groups, demographics, and geographic regions. This allows businesses to target their ideal audience and reach potential customers effectively.

b) High Engagement: TikTok's immersive and addictive nature keeps users engaged for extended periods. This high level of engagement translates into increased visibility and greater opportunities for brands to connect with their target audience.

c) Creative Opportunities: TikTok's emphasis on creative expression opens up a world of possibilities for brands to create unique and engaging ad campaigns. From catchy music-driven ads to viral challenges, TikTok provides a platform for brands to showcase their creativity and establish a strong brand identity.

d) Viral Potential: TikTok's viral nature enables content to spread rapidly across the platform. A well-executed ad campaign has the potential to go viral, gaining exposure to millions of users and generating organic buzz for your brand.

e) Influencer Marketing: TikTok is home to a vast community of influencers who have built loyal followings. Partnering with influencers can amplify your brand's reach, increase credibility, and generate authentic engagement with your target audience.

1.3 Types of TikTok Ads Available

TikTok offers a range of ad formats tailored to different marketing objectives. Here are some of the popular types of TikTok ads:

a) In-Feed Ads: These ads appear seamlessly within users' "For You" feeds, blending with organic content. They can include images, videos, or carousel formats, allowing brands to showcase their products, services, or stories in a visually appealing manner.

b) Brand Takeover Ads: These ads are full-screen ads that appear immediately when users open the TikTok app. They are highly impactful and enable brands to capture users' attention right from the start.

c) Branded Hashtag Challenges: This ad format encourages user participation by creating a challenge around a branded hashtag. It invites users to create and share content related to the challenge, creating a wave of user-generated content and increasing brand visibility.

d) TopView Ads: Similar to Brand Takeover Ads, TopView Ads are full-screen, but they appear after a user has been on the app for a short period. These ads provide an excellent opportunity for brands to deliver their message to engaged users.

e) Branded Effects: TikTok offers branded effects, which are custom filters, stickers, or special effects that users can apply to their videos. Brands can create their own branded effects, allowing users to engage with their brand in a fun and interactive way.

Understanding the various types of TikTok ads available will help you choose the most suitable format for your marketing goals and create impactful campaigns that

Chapter 2: Getting Started with TikTok Ads

In this chapter, I will guide you through the process of getting started with TikTok Ads. We'll cover everything from creating a TikTok Ads Manager account to setting up your first ad campaign. Additionally, we'll explore the importance of defining your advertising objectives and target audience. Let's begin!

2.1 Creating a TikTok Ads Manager Account

To get started with TikTok Ads, you'll need to create an account on TikTok Ads Manager. Here's a step-by-step guide:

a) Visit the TikTok Ads Manager website (ads.tiktok.com) and click on the "Create an Ad" button.

b) You'll be prompted to log in to your TikTok account. If you don't have one, sign up for a TikTok account first.

c) Once logged in, click on the "Create" button in the top right corner and select "Campaign" from the dropdown menu.

d) Choose your objective for the ad campaign, such as increasing brand awareness, driving website traffic, or promoting app installs.

e) Provide the necessary details for your campaign, including the campaign name, budget, and schedule.

f) Click on "Next" to proceed to the Ad Group level, where you'll define your target audience, placements, and budget allocation.

g) Finally, proceed to the Ad level, where you'll create your actual ad by selecting the ad format, uploading creative assets, and adding a compelling ad copy.

2.2 Setting up Your TikTok Ad Campaign

When setting up your TikTok ad campaign, it's crucial to define your campaign structure and objectives clearly. Here are some key steps to consider:

a) Campaign Structure: Determine the structure of your campaign by organizing your ads into different ad groups. This allows you to manage and optimize specific targeting and budget settings for each ad group.

b) Objective Selection: Choose the most relevant objective for your campaign. TikTok offers various objectives, including brand awareness, reach, traffic, app installs, conversions, and more. Select the objective that aligns with your marketing goals.

c) Budgeting and Schedule: Set your campaign budget and schedule. Decide how much you are willing to spend on your ad campaign and allocate your budget based on daily or lifetime spending. Additionally, set the start and end dates for your campaign.

d) Targeting Options: TikTok provides several targeting options to help you reach your desired audience. You can target based on demographics (age, gender, location), interests, behaviors, and even specific devices. Utilize these options to narrow down your audience and increase the effectiveness of your ads.

2.3 Defining Your Advertising Objectives and Target Audience

Before launching your TikTok ad campaign, it's crucial to define your advertising objectives and target audience. This step sets the foundation for a successful campaign. Consider the following:

a) Advertising Objectives: Clearly define what you want to achieve with your TikTok ad campaign. Is it to raise brand awareness, drive sales, generate leads, or increase app installs? Having a clear objective will guide your ad strategy and help you measure success.

b) Target Audience: Understand your target audience and their preferences. Consider factors such as age, gender, location, interests, and behaviors. Conduct thorough market research and leverage audience insights provided by TikTok Ads Manager to refine your targeting and tailor your ads to resonate with your audience.

c) Persona Development: Create detailed buyer personas to represent your target audience segments. These personas will help you understand your audience's needs, motivations, pain points, and preferred content formats. Craft your ads to align with these personas to increase engagement and conversions.

By carefully defining your advertising objectives and target audience, you'll be able to create highly relevant and targeted TikTok ad campaigns.

Chapter 3: Crafting Compelling TikTok Ads

In this chapter, we will explore the art of crafting compelling TikTok ads that captivate your audience and drive results. We'll discuss the various TikTok ad formats, share best practices for creating attention-grabbing ads, delve into storytelling techniques for maximum impact, and explore how to incorporate trends and challenges into your ads. Let's get started!

3.1 Understanding the TikTok Ad Formats

TikTok offers a variety of ad formats to suit different marketing objectives and creative styles. Familiarize yourself with these ad formats to choose the most suitable one for your campaign:

a) In-Feed Ads: These ads appear seamlessly in users' "For You" feed, similar to organic TikTok content. In-Feed Ads can include images, videos, or carousel formats and provide an excellent opportunity to showcase your brand, products, or services.

b) Brand Takeover Ads: Brand Takeover Ads are full-screen ads that appear immediately when users open the TikTok app. These ads have high visibility and are effective for capturing users' attention right from the start.

c) Branded Hashtag Challenges: This ad format encourages user participation by creating a challenge around a branded hashtag. Users are invited to create and share content related to the challenge, generating user-generated content and increasing brand visibility.

d) TopView Ads: Similar to Brand Takeover Ads, TopView Ads are full-screen ads that appear after a user has been on the app for a short period. These ads provide an excellent opportunity for brands to deliver their message to engaged users.

e) Branded Effects: TikTok offers branded effects, which are custom filters, stickers, or special effects that users can apply to their videos. Brands can create their own branded effects, allowing users to engage with their brand in a fun and interactive way.

3.2 Best Practices for Creating Attention-Grabbing Ads

To create TikTok ads that capture users' attention and make a lasting impression, consider the following best practices:

a) Keep it Short and Snappy: TikTok's format revolves around short-form videos, so ensure that your ads are concise and engaging. Grab users' attention within the first few seconds and deliver your message quickly.

b) Use Eye-Catching Visuals: TikTok is a visually-driven platform, so focus on creating visually appealing ads. Use high-quality images or videos that align with your brand identity and resonate with your target audience.

c) Leverage Captions and Text: While TikTok is primarily a visual platform, including captions and text can enhance your message and make it more accessible. Use clear and concise captions that convey your brand's key message effectively.

d) Incorporate Music and Sound: Music plays a significant role in TikTok culture. Choose catchy and upbeat soundtracks that align with your ad's mood and theme. Incorporate sound effects or voiceovers to add an extra layer of engagement.

3.3 Storytelling Techniques for Maximum Impact

Storytelling is a powerful tool for connecting with your audience on TikTok. Consider these storytelling techniques to create impactful ads:

a) Emotionally Engage: Use storytelling to evoke emotions and create a connection with your audience. Tap into relatable experiences or address pain points that your target audience can identify with.

b) Show, Don't Tell: Instead of directly promoting your product or service, show how it can enhance users' lives. Demonstrate the benefits and features through compelling visual narratives.

c) Be Authentic and Relatable: TikTok thrives on authenticity. Craft ads that feel genuine and relatable to your target audience. Incorporate real people, user-generated content, or testimonials to build trust.

3.4 Incorporating Trends and Challenges into Your Ads

TikTok is known for its viral trends and challenges. Leveraging these trends and challenges in your TikTok ads can help increase engagement and brand exposure. Here's how you can incorporate them effectively:

a) Stay Current: Keep a close eye on the trending hashtags, challenges, and popular content formats on TikTok. Stay up to date with the latest viral trends to ensure your ads are relevant and resonate with the TikTok community.

b) Participate in Challenges: Consider participating in existing challenges or creating your branded hashtag challenge. Align the challenge with your brand values and products, encouraging users to create content that showcases your brand.

c) Collaborate with TikTok Influencers: Partnering with popular TikTok influencers who are active participants in challenges can give your ads a boost. Influencers can create authentic content that incorporates your brand and challenge, reaching their dedicated fanbase.

d) Be Creative and Unique: While it's essential to stay on-trend, add your unique twist to stand out from the crowd. Infuse your brand's creativity and personality into the challenge or trend, making it memorable for viewers.

e) Encourage User-Generated Content (UGC): Create ads that inspire users to generate their content related to the challenge or trend. User-generated content not only builds brand engagement but also amplifies your brand's reach as users share their creations.

Remember to be strategic in your approach when incorporating trends and challenges into your ads. Ensure that they align with your brand identity, resonate with your target audience, and support your overall advertising objectives.

By understanding the TikTok ad formats, implementing best practices for attention-grabbing ads, incorporating storytelling techniques, and leveraging trends and challenges, you can create compelling TikTok ads that resonate with your audience, drive engagement, and maximize your advertising impact.

Chapter 4: Targeting and Audience Segmentation

In this chapter, we will explore the importance of targeting and audience segmentation in TikTok Ads. We'll discuss how to leverage TikTok's targeting options, define your ideal target audience, create custom audiences for precise targeting, and utilize the TikTok pixel for tracking and retargeting. Let's dive in!

4.1 Leveraging TikTok's Targeting Options

TikTok offers a range of targeting options to help you reach your desired audience effectively. Here are some key targeting options to consider:

a) Demographics: Narrow down your audience based on demographics such as age, gender, location, language, and device type. This allows you to target specific groups that align with your product or service.

b) Interests and Behaviors: Target users based on their interests, hobbies, and behaviors. TikTok analyzes user behavior and engagement to understand their preferences and deliver relevant ads.

c) Custom Audiences: Utilize custom audiences to target users who have already interacted with your brand. This includes website visitors, app users, customer lists, or engagement with your TikTok content.

d) Lookalike Audiences: Expand your reach by targeting users who have similar characteristics to your existing customer base. TikTok's algorithm analyzes your custom audience to find similar profiles for effective targeting.

e) Retargeting: Retarget users who have previously engaged with your ads or visited your website. This helps to reinforce your message and increase the likelihood of conversion.

4.2 Defining Your Ideal Target Audience

Before launching your TikTok ad campaign, it's crucial to define your ideal target audience. Consider the following steps to define your audience effectively:

a) Conduct Market Research: Gain insights into your target market by conducting thorough market research. Understand their demographics, preferences, behaviors, and pain points. This information will guide your targeting strategy.

b) Develop Buyer Personas: Create detailed buyer personas that represent your ideal customers. Consider factors such as age, gender, occupation, interests, motivations, and challenges. This helps you tailor your ads to resonate with specific audience segments.

c) Align with Brand Values: Identify the values and aspirations of your brand. This will help attract an audience that aligns with your brand identity and is more likely to engage with your ads.

d) Test and Refine: Launch your ads to a broad audience initially and analyze the performance metrics. Use this data to refine your targeting strategy, focusing on the segments that show the most engagement and conversions.

4.3 Creating Custom Audiences for Precise Targeting

Custom audiences allow you to target specific groups of users who have interacted with your brand in some way. Here's how you can create custom audiences for precise targeting on TikTok:

a) Website Custom Audiences: Install the TikTok pixel on your website to track user behavior. This allows you to create custom audiences based on specific actions, such as page visits, add to cart, or purchase.

b) App Custom Audiences: Integrate the TikTok SDK into your mobile app to track user interactions. Create custom audiences based on in-app actions, such as app installs, in-app purchases, or specific events.

c) Customer List Custom Audiences: Upload customer lists containing email addresses or mobile advertising IDs. TikTok matches the uploaded data with its user base, enabling you to target your existing customers or prospects.

d) Engagement Custom Audiences: Create custom audiences based on user engagement with your TikTok content. This includes users who have watched your videos, liked, shared, or commented on them.

4.4 Using TikTok Pixel for Tracking and Retargeting

The TikTok pixel is a tracking tool that helps you measure the effectiveness of your ad campaigns and retarget users who have interacted with your website. Here's how you can use the TikTok pixel for tracking and retargeting:

a) Install the TikTok Pixel: To start using the TikTok pixel, you'll need to install it on your website. Access the pixel code from the TikTok Ads Manager and place it on all pages of your website.

b) Track Conversions: The TikTok pixel allows you to track various conversion events on your website, such as purchases, sign-ups, or form submissions. Set up the pixel to track these events, enabling you to measure the effectiveness of your ad campaigns and optimize for better results.

c) Create Custom Audiences: With the TikTok pixel installed, you can create custom audiences based on user interactions with your website. For example, you can create an audience of users who have added items to their cart but haven't made a purchase. This enables you to retarget these users with relevant ads to encourage them to complete their purchase.

d) Retargeting Campaigns: Use the custom audiences you've created to launch retargeting campaigns. Show ads specifically to users who have previously visited your website or performed specific actions. This helps keep your brand top of mind and encourages users to re-engage with your products or services.

e) Lookalike Audiences: The TikTok pixel can also be used to create lookalike audiences. By analyzing the behavior of users who have interacted with your website, the pixel can find similar profiles within the TikTok user base. Targeting these lookalike audiences allows you to reach new potential customers who share characteristics with your existing audience.

f) Conversion Optimization: The TikTok pixel provides valuable data for optimizing your ad campaigns. By tracking conversions, you can leverage TikTok's conversion optimization feature, which automatically delivers your ads to users who are most likely to take the desired action on your website. This improves the efficiency and effectiveness of your campaigns.

Remember to comply with privacy regulations and ensure you have proper consent mechanisms in place when utilizing tracking pixels and collecting user data.

By leveraging TikTok's targeting options, defining your ideal target audience, creating custom audiences, and using the TikTok pixel for tracking and retargeting, you can optimize your TikTok ad campaigns to reach the right users at the right time, maximizing your advertising success.

Chapter 5: Optimizing TikTok Ad Campaigns

In this chapter, we will explore the key strategies and techniques for optimizing TikTok ad campaigns. We'll discuss how to analyze and interpret campaign metrics, conduct A/B testing for ad performance optimization, improve click-through rates (CTR) and conversion rates, and implement effective budgeting and bidding strategies. Let's dive in!

5.1 Analyzing and Interpreting Campaign Metrics

Analyzing campaign metrics is crucial for understanding the performance of your TikTok ad campaigns. Here are some key metrics to track and interpret:

a) Impressions: The number of times your ad was displayed to users.

b) Clicks: The number of times users clicked on your ad.

c) Click-through Rate (CTR): The percentage of users who clicked on your ad after seeing it. It is calculated by dividing the number of clicks by the number of impressions and multiplying by 100.

d) Engagement Metrics: Measure metrics such as video views, likes, comments, and shares to gauge the level of user engagement with your ads.

e) Conversion Metrics: Track conversion events such as purchases, sign-ups, or downloads to assess the effectiveness of your campaigns in driving desired actions.

f) Return on Ad Spend (ROAS): Calculate the revenue generated from your ad campaigns divided by the total ad spend. ROAS helps determine the profitability of your campaigns.

Regularly monitor these metrics, identify trends, and make data-driven decisions to optimize your campaigns for better performance.

5.2 A/B Testing for Ad Performance Optimization

A/B testing involves comparing two or more variations of an ad to identify which performs better. Here's how you can conduct A/B testing for ad performance optimization:

a) Define Test Variables: Select specific elements to test, such as ad creatives, ad copy, call-to-action buttons, or landing pages.

b) Create Variations: Develop multiple versions of your ad, each with a single variable changed. For example, test different images, headlines, or video lengths.

c) Split Ad Groups: Divide your target audience into different ad groups, assigning each group to one variation of the ad.

d) Track and Compare Performance: Measure the performance of each variation by monitoring the relevant metrics. Identify the winning variation based on the desired outcome, such as higher CTR or conversion rate.

e) Iterate and Optimize: Apply the insights gained from the A/B test to optimize your future ad campaigns. Implement the winning elements and continue testing to refine your strategies further.

5.3 Strategies for Improving Click-through Rates (CTR) and Conversion Rates

A high CTR and conversion rate are indicators of an effective ad campaign. Here are some strategies to improve these rates:

a) Compelling Ad Creatives: Create visually appealing and engaging ads that capture users' attention. Use vibrant colors, eye-catching visuals, and clear messaging to entice users to click on your ad.

b) Clear Call-to-Action (CTA): Include a clear and compelling CTA in your ad copy. Encourage users to take action by using action-oriented language and highlighting the benefits they will receive.

c) Ad Relevance: Ensure that your ads align with users' interests and motivations. Target specific audience segments with personalized messaging to increase relevance and engagement.

d) Landing Page Optimization: Ensure your landing pages are optimized for conversion. Provide a seamless user experience, clear value proposition, and easy-to-complete forms to facilitate user actions.

e) Ad Placement and Timing: Experiment with different ad placements and timings to identify the most effective combination for your target audience. Test placements within the TikTok feed, specific categories, or during peak user activity times.

5.4 Budgeting and Bidding Strategies

Effective budgeting and bidding strategies help you optimize your ad spend and maximize your campaign results.

Here are some budgeting and bidding strategies to consider:

a) Set Clear Objectives: Define your advertising objectives and align your budget accordingly. Determine whether your goal is to increase brand awareness, drive website traffic, or generate conversions. This clarity will guide your budget allocation.

b) Start with a Test Budget: When launching a new campaign or testing new ad formats, start with a smaller test budget to gather data and evaluate performance. This allows you to make informed decisions before scaling up.

c) Monitor Cost Metrics: Keep a close eye on cost metrics such as Cost per Click (CPC), Cost per Thousand Impressions (CPM), and Cost per Acquisition (CPA). Analyze these metrics to ensure you are maximizing the value of your budget and adjusting bids if necessary.

d) Bid Optimization: TikTok offers bidding options such as Target Cost, Maximum Bid, and Enhanced Cost per Click (eCPC). Test different bidding strategies to find the most effective approach for your campaigns. Consider using automated bidding options to optimize your bids based on your specified goals.

e) Campaign Performance Analysis: Regularly review the performance of your campaigns and adjust your budget allocation accordingly. Allocate more budget to campaigns that are generating positive results and consider reducing budget for underperforming campaigns.

f) Scaling Successful Campaigns: Once you identify successful campaigns that are delivering the desired results, consider scaling them up by increasing your budget. Monitor the scalability and maintain a balance between budget allocation and campaign performance.

g) Lifetime and Daily Budgeting: Choose between lifetime and daily budgeting based on your campaign goals and budget constraints. Lifetime budgeting allows you to set a total budget for the entire campaign duration, while daily budgeting allows you to allocate a specific budget for each day.

h) Regular Optimization: Continuously optimize your campaigns based on performance insights. Adjust your budget, targeting, and ad creatives to improve ROI and achieve your campaign objectives.

Remember that budgeting and bidding strategies may require iteration and refinement over time. Stay vigilant, monitor performance, and adapt your strategies as needed to optimize your TikTok ad campaigns.

By analyzing and interpreting campaign metrics, conducting A/B testing, improving click-through rates and conversion rates, and implementing effective budgeting and bidding strategies, you can optimize your TikTok ad campaigns to drive better results and maximize your return on investment.

Chapter 6: Advanced TikTok Advertising Strategies

In this chapter, we will explore advanced TikTok advertising strategies that can take your campaigns to the next level. We'll discuss influencer marketing on TikTok, collaborating with TikTok creators and influencers, leveraging TikTok's brand partnerships and branded effects, and cross-promoting TikTok ads on other platforms. Let's dive in!

6.1 Influencer Marketing on TikTok

Influencer marketing is a powerful strategy to reach and engage with your target audience on TikTok. Influencers have established credibility and a dedicated following, making them effective partners for promoting your brand. Here's how you can leverage influencer marketing on TikTok:

a) Identify Relevant Influencers: Research and identify influencers who align with your brand values, target audience, and campaign objectives. Look for influencers who have a substantial following and high engagement rates.

b) Authentic Collaborations: Approach influencers with collaboration proposals that align with their content style and resonate with their audience. Encourage them to create authentic and engaging content that showcases your brand in a natural and relatable way.

c) Sponsored Content: Collaborate with influencers to create sponsored content that promotes your products, services, or brand message. Allow influencers creative freedom while ensuring the content aligns with your brand guidelines and objectives.

d) Hashtag Challenges: Leverage influencer partnerships to launch branded hashtag challenges. Influencers can kick-start the challenge, encouraging their followers to participate and create user-generated content related to your brand.

e) Track Performance: Monitor the performance of influencer campaigns by tracking metrics such as engagement, reach, and conversions. Use this data to evaluate the success of the collaborations and make informed decisions for future partnerships.

6.2 Collaborating with TikTok Creators and Influencers

TikTok creators and influencers have a deep understanding of the platform's dynamics and can create content that resonates with their followers. Collaborating with them can help amplify your brand's reach and engagement. Consider the following when collaborating with TikTok creators and influencers:

a) Research and Outreach: Research TikTok creators who produce content relevant to your industry or target audience. Reach out to them with collaboration proposals that showcase how your brand aligns with their content style and interests.

b) Co-Creation: Foster a collaborative relationship with TikTok creators by involving them in the creative process. Work together to develop content ideas that authentically incorporate your brand while staying true to their unique style.

c) Branded Content Deals: Consider offering branded content deals to TikTok creators. This can involve a long-term partnership or a series of sponsored content collaborations. Negotiate terms such as content frequency, exclusivity, and compensation based on the influencer's reach and engagement.

d) Content Amplification: Once the collaboration is live, encourage the TikTok creator to promote the content on their other social media platforms. This cross-promotion can help expand the reach of your TikTok ads to a broader audience.

e) Maintain Relationships: Cultivate relationships with TikTok creators and influencers for ongoing collaborations. By nurturing these partnerships, you can tap into their creativity and influence to continuously enhance your TikTok advertising efforts.

6.3 Leveraging TikTok's Brand Partnerships and Branded Effects

TikTok offers brand partnerships and branded effects that can help increase brand visibility and engagement. Here's how you can leverage these features:

a) Brand Partnerships: Explore TikTok's brand partnership opportunities, such as branded hashtags, brand takeovers, or in-feed ads. These partnerships allow you to collaborate directly with TikTok to create unique ad experiences that align with your brand's objectives.

b) Branded Effects: TikTok offers various branded effects, including filters, stickers, and AR effects. Create custom branded effects that users can apply to their videos, allowing them to immerse themselves in your brand's experience. Branded effects can help generate user-generated content and increase brand awareness.

c) Hashtag Challenges Plus: TikTok's Hashtag Challenges Plus feature allows you to combine branded effects and a branded hashtag challenge. This integration enhances user engagement by providing a seamless and immersive brand experience.

d) Sponsored Hashtag Challenges: TikTok offers sponsored hashtag challenges, where brands can sponsor a specific hashtag challenge to gain exposure and encourage user participation. Collaborate with TikTok to create a unique challenge that aligns with your brand and encourages user-generated content.

e) Co-Branded Content: Partner with TikTok influencers, creators, or celebrities to co-create branded content that showcases your products or services. This collaboration can help amplify your brand's reach and credibility.

6.4 Cross-Promoting TikTok Ads on Other Platforms

To maximize the impact of your TikTok ad campaigns, consider cross-promoting your TikTok ads on other social media platforms. This approach allows you to extend your reach beyond TikTok's user base and target users on multiple platforms. Here's how you can cross-promote your TikTok ads:

a) Repurpose TikTok Content: Adapt and repurpose your TikTok ad content for other platforms such as Instagram, Facebook, or YouTube. Tailor the content format and length to suit the specific requirements of each platform while maintaining the essence of your TikTok ad.

b) Share Highlights and Teasers: Create highlights or teasers of your TikTok ad campaigns to generate interest and curiosity. Share these snippets on other social media platforms, directing users to view the full ad on TikTok.

c) Influencer Collaborations: Collaborate with influencers or content creators on other platforms to promote your TikTok ads. They can share snippets of your TikTok ad or create content around your brand that encourages their followers to engage with your TikTok campaign.

d) Cross-Platform Ad Campaigns: Consider running coordinated ad campaigns across multiple platforms. Create a cohesive narrative and consistent visual identity to reinforce your brand message and increase brand recognition.

e) Leverage Email Marketing: If you have an email subscriber list, include links or embed TikTok ad content in your email newsletters to promote your campaigns. This allows you to reach your existing audience and drive them to engage with your TikTok content.

By incorporating influencer marketing, collaborating with TikTok creators, leveraging TikTok's brand partnerships and branded effects, and cross-promoting TikTok ads on other platforms, you can extend your brand's reach, engagement, and impact, maximizing the effectiveness of your TikTok advertising efforts.

Remember to align your collaborations, partnerships, and cross-promotions with your overall marketing objectives and target audience to ensure consistency and effectiveness across platforms.

Chapter 7: Overcoming Challenges and Pitfalls

In this chapter, we will discuss common challenges and pitfalls that advertisers may encounter when running TikTok ad campaigns. We'll provide strategies and tips for dealing with ad fatigue, adapting to algorithm changes and trends, avoiding common mistakes, and managing negative feedback and comments. Let's explore how to overcome these challenges effectively.

7.1 Dealing with Ad Fatigue and Banner Blindness

Ad fatigue occurs when your target audience becomes disengaged or indifferent towards your ads due to repeated exposure. Banner blindness, on the other hand, refers to users ignoring or disregarding banner-like ads. Here's how you can overcome these challenges:

a) Refresh Your Ad Creatives: Regularly update and refresh your ad creatives to maintain user interest.

Experiment with different visuals, messaging, and formats to keep your ads fresh and engaging.

b) Rotate Ad Variations: Instead of repeatedly showing the same ad to your audience, create multiple variations of your ad and rotate them to avoid monotony. This approach helps maintain user engagement and prevents ad fatigue.

c) Test Different Ad Formats: Explore various ad formats offered by TikTok, such as in-feed ads, branded effects, or top view ads. Testing different formats can capture users' attention and prevent banner blindness.

d) Use Frequency Capping: Set frequency caps to limit the number of times an individual user sees your ad within a specific time period. This prevents overexposure and reduces the risk of ad fatigue.

e) Target Specific Audience Segments: Refine your targeting strategy to reach specific audience segments within your target market. By narrowing down your audience, you can deliver more relevant ads, minimizing the chances of ad fatigue.

7.2 Adapting to Algorithm Changes and Trends

TikTok's algorithm continually evolves, and staying updated with these changes is crucial for the success of your ad campaigns. Additionally, staying in tune with the latest trends can help you align your content with what's popular on the platform. Consider the following strategies:

a) Stay Informed: Keep up-to-date with TikTok's algorithm changes, new features, and updates. Follow TikTok's official announcements, read industry blogs, and engage in relevant communities to stay informed.

b) Monitor Trending Content: Regularly browse TikTok to identify emerging trends, hashtags, and challenges that align with your brand. Incorporate these trends into your ad campaigns to leverage the platform's viral nature and increase engagement.

c) Be Agile: Be prepared to adapt your ad creatives and strategies based on algorithm changes and trends. Stay flexible and responsive to the evolving landscape of TikTok to maximize your campaign's effectiveness.

d) Test and Experiment: Continuously test different approaches, ad formats, and content styles to identify what works best for your target audience. Experimentation allows you to uncover new opportunities and adapt to changes quickly.

7.3 Avoiding Common Mistakes in TikTok Ad Campaigns

To run successful TikTok ad campaigns, it's essential to avoid common mistakes that can hinder your results. Here are a few pitfalls to watch out for:

a) Lack of Audience Research: Ensure you have a deep understanding of your target audience's demographics, interests, and behaviors. Conduct thorough audience research to tailor your ads effectively.

b) Inconsistent Branding: Maintain consistent branding across your TikTok ads and other marketing channels. Inconsistent branding can confuse users and weaken your brand's identity.

c) Poor Ad Relevance: Ensure your ads are relevant to the target audience and the context of the platform.

Irrelevant or out-of-context ads may not resonate with users and lead to poor engagement.

d) Ignoring Analytics and Metrics: Regularly monitor and analyze your campaign metrics to gain insights into what's working and what needs improvement. Ignoring data and metrics can prevent you from making informed decisions and optimizing your TikTok ad campaigns.

e) Neglecting Creative Quality: Invest in high-quality ad creatives that capture attention and convey your brand message effectively. Poorly designed or low-quality ads can negatively impact user perception and engagement.

f) Overcomplicating Your Message: Keep your ad messaging clear, concise, and easy to understand. Avoid overloading your audience with excessive information or complex messaging that may confuse or disengage them.

g) Lack of Call-to-Action (CTA): Include a clear and compelling CTA in your ads to guide users towards the desired action, whether it's visiting your website, making a purchase, or downloading an app. A strong CTA improves conversion rates and drives user engagement.

7.4 Managing Negative Feedback and Comments

TikTok, like any other social media platform, may invite negative feedback or comments on your ads. Here's how you can effectively manage and address them:

a) Stay Responsive: Monitor the comments section of your ads and respond promptly to user feedback. Address concerns, provide assistance, and engage in a respectful and professional manner.

b) Handle Criticism Professionally: Remain composed and professional when responding to negative comments or criticism. Avoid engaging in heated debates or responding defensively. Instead, offer solutions or seek to understand and resolve any issues.

c) Use Filters and Moderation Tools: TikTok provides moderation tools that allow you to filter and block inappropriate or spam comments. Utilize these tools to maintain a positive and safe environment for your ad campaigns.

d) Encourage Positive Engagement: Encourage positive engagement by responding to positive comments and expressing gratitude. This helps foster a positive brand image and encourages others to engage positively as well.

e) Learn from Feedback: Use negative feedback as an opportunity for growth and improvement. Analyze user feedback to identify areas where you can enhance your ad campaigns or address any shortcomings.

f) Seek Help if Necessary: If you encounter persistent negative feedback or online harassment, consider reaching out to TikTok's support or community management team for assistance in resolving the issue.

By proactively addressing ad fatigue and banner blindness, adapting to algorithm changes and trends, avoiding common mistakes, and effectively managing negative feedback and comments, you can navigate challenges and optimize your TikTok ad campaigns for better results.

Remember, maintaining a positive and engaging presence on TikTok contributes to building brand loyalty and fostering a favorable brand perception among users.

Chapter 8: Legal and Ethical Considerations

In this chapter, we will discuss the legal and ethical considerations you need to keep in mind when running TikTok ad campaigns. Adhering to TikTok's advertising policies and guidelines, ensuring compliance with local regulations and laws, and prioritizing user privacy and data security are essential. Let's explore these considerations in more detail.

8.1 Adhering to TikTok's Advertising Policies and Guidelines

TikTok has specific advertising policies and guidelines that govern what types of ads are allowed on the platform. It's crucial to familiarize yourself with these policies and ensure that your ads comply with them. Here are some key areas to consider:

a) Prohibited Content: Understand the types of content that TikTok prohibits in their ads, such as illegal substances, adult content, hate speech, or misleading claims. Ensure that your ads align with TikTok's content guidelines.

b) Creative Restrictions: TikTok may have specific guidelines regarding the use of copyrighted material, trademarks, or sensitive topics. Respect these restrictions and avoid any infringement or violation of intellectual property rights.

c) Age-Restricted Content: If your ads are targeted towards specific age groups, ensure that you comply with TikTok's guidelines for age-restricted content. Adhere to age-appropriate content and follow the necessary age verification procedures.

d) Transparency and Disclosure: Clearly disclose any sponsored content or promotions in your ads. Transparency is essential to maintain the trust of TikTok users and comply with advertising regulations.

8.2 Ensuring Compliance with Local Regulations and Laws

Apart from TikTok's policies, it's important to comply with local regulations and laws governing advertising practices in your target markets. Consider the following aspects:

a) Advertising Standards: Familiarize yourself with the advertising standards and regulations specific to the regions where you run your TikTok ad campaigns. These regulations may cover areas such as truth in advertising, comparative advertising, and endorsements.

b) Product-Specific Regulations: If you are advertising products or services that are subject to specific regulations (e.g., pharmaceuticals, alcohol, or financial services), ensure compliance with the relevant industry regulations and requirements.

c) Data Protection and Privacy: Respect user privacy and adhere to data protection regulations. Obtain proper consent for data collection and ensure that you handle user data securely and in accordance with applicable privacy laws.

d) Influencer Marketing Guidelines: If you engage in influencer marketing on TikTok, be aware of the guidelines and regulations that govern this practice. Ensure that influencers disclose their partnerships with your brand and comply with relevant advertising standards.

8.3 Protecting User Privacy and Data Security

User privacy and data security should be a top priority when running TikTok ad campaigns. Safeguarding user information builds trust and helps maintain a positive brand image. Consider the following practices:

a) Obtain User Consent: If you collect any personal data from TikTok users through your ad campaigns, ensure that you have obtained proper consent. Clearly communicate how the data will be used and give users the option to opt out if desired.

b) Secure Data Handling: Implement robust data security measures to protect user data from unauthorized access, loss, or misuse. Encrypt sensitive data, follow secure data storage practices, and regularly assess and update your security protocols.

c) Transparent Data Practices: Be transparent about how you collect, use, and store user data. Clearly outline your data practices in your privacy policy and provide users with accessible information on their rights and options.

d) Ad Personalization and Retargeting: If you engage in ad personalization or retargeting based on user data, ensure that you comply with privacy regulations and respect user preferences. Provide clear options for users to manage their ad preferences or opt out of personalized ads.

e) Compliance with TikTok's Data Policies: Familiarize yourself with TikTok's data policies and ensure that your data collection and handling practices align with their guidelines. TikTok has specific rules regarding the use of user data, so it's important to understand and comply with these policies.

f) Third-Party Data Partners: If you work with third-party data partners or providers, ensure that they adhere to privacy regulations and have appropriate data protection measures in place. Conduct due diligence when selecting and engaging with these partners.

g) Data Retention and Deletion: Define data retention periods and establish procedures for deleting user data when it's no longer necessary or requested by users. Regularly review and update your data retention practices to comply with applicable regulations.

h) User Rights and Requests: Respect user rights regarding their data. Provide mechanisms for users to access, rectify, or delete their data as required by data protection laws. Respond promptly and appropriately to user requests related to their data.

By adhering to TikTok's advertising policies, complying with local regulations and laws, and prioritizing user privacy and data security, you can ensure that your TikTok ad campaigns are conducted in an ethical and legally compliant manner.

It's recommended to consult with legal professionals or experts in advertising regulations and data protection to ensure that your campaigns align with the specific requirements of your target markets. Stay updated on changes in regulations and periodically review and adapt your practices to remain in compliance with the evolving legal landscape.

Chapter 9: Measuring Success and ROI

In this chapter, we will explore the essential aspects of measuring the success and return on investment (ROI) of your TikTok ad campaigns. By identifying key performance indicators (KPIs), tracking conversions, evaluating ROI, and continuously iterating your advertising strategy, you can optimize your campaigns for maximum effectiveness. Let's delve into these topics further.

9.1 Key Performance Indicators (KPIs) for TikTok Ad Campaigns

To gauge the performance and success of your TikTok ad campaigns, it's important to define and track relevant KPIs. The choice of KPIs may vary depending on your campaign objectives, but here are some common ones to consider:

a) Impressions: The number of times your ad is shown to TikTok users.

b) Click-Through Rate (CTR): The percentage of users who click on your ad after seeing it. It indicates ad engagement and interest.

c) Conversion Rate: The percentage of users who complete a desired action, such as making a purchase or filling out a form, after clicking on your ad.

d) Cost per Result: The average cost you incur for each desired action or conversion.

e) Return on Ad Spend (ROAS): The revenue generated compared to the amount spent on advertising. It helps assess the profitability of your ad campaigns.

f) Engagement Metrics: Metrics such as likes, comments, shares, and video completion rates that indicate user engagement and interaction with your ads.

g) Reach and Frequency: The number of unique users reached by your ads and the average number of times they are exposed to your ads, respectively.

h) Brand Awareness Metrics: Assessing metrics related to brand recall, sentiment, or recognition to measure the impact on brand awareness.

Identify the most relevant KPIs based on your campaign objectives and regularly track them to monitor the performance and effectiveness of your TikTok ad campaigns.

9.2 Tracking Conversions and Attributing Results

To accurately measure the impact of your TikTok ad campaigns, it's essential to implement proper tracking and attribution methods. Here are some strategies to consider:

a) TikTok Pixel: Implement the TikTok Pixel—a tracking code provided by TikTok—on your website or landing pages. The Pixel allows you to track conversions, measure performance, and optimize your campaigns.

b) Conversion Tracking: Define and track specific conversion events, such as purchases, sign-ups, or downloads, using the TikTok Pixel. Set up conversion tracking to attribute these actions to your ad campaigns accurately.

c) UTM Parameters: Use UTM parameters in your ad URLs to track traffic sources and campaign-specific data in your analytics tools. This enables you to attribute conversions to specific TikTok ad campaigns or placements.

d) Multi-Touch Attribution: Consider employing multi-touch attribution models to understand the contribution of each touchpoint in the user journey. It helps you assess the impact of TikTok ads throughout the customer conversion path.

e) A/B Testing: Conduct A/B tests with different ad variations to identify the most effective elements and optimize your campaigns based on data-driven insights.

Accurate tracking and attribution allow you to understand the impact of your TikTok ad campaigns on conversions and optimize your advertising strategy accordingly.

9.3 Evaluating the Return on Investment (ROI)

Measuring the ROI of your TikTok ad campaigns helps you assess their profitability and make informed decisions. Here's how you can evaluate ROI effectively:

a) Define ROI Metrics: Determine the specific metrics you will use to calculate ROI, such as revenue generated, customer acquisition costs, or lifetime value of customers.

b) Calculate Costs: Calculate the total costs incurred for your TikTok ad campaigns, including ad spend, creative production, and any additional expenses.

c) Measure Revenue: Measure the revenue directly attributed to your TikTok ad campaigns. This can be done by tracking conversions and attributing them to your campaigns using the methods discussed earlier.

d) Calculate ROI: Once you have the total costs and revenue, calculate the ROI using the following formula:

$$ROI = ((Revenue - Costs) / Costs) * 100$$

The ROI will provide you with a percentage that represents the return on investment for your TikTok ad campaigns. A positive ROI indicates a profitable campaign, while a negative ROI means that the campaign did not generate sufficient revenue to cover the costs.

e) Evaluate ROI Across Campaigns: Compare the ROI of different TikTok ad campaigns to identify the most successful ones. This analysis can help you understand which campaigns are delivering the highest return and allocate your resources accordingly.

9.4 Iterating and Refining Your Advertising Strategy

Measuring success and ROI is not just about assessing past performance but also using the insights gained to refine and optimize your future TikTok ad campaigns. Here are some strategies for iterating and refining your advertising strategy:

a) Analyze Performance Data: Regularly review and analyze the performance data of your TikTok ad campaigns. Look for patterns, trends, and areas for improvement. Identify campaigns or ad variations that are underperforming and determine ways to enhance their effectiveness.

b) Experiment with Different Strategies: Continuously test and experiment with different ad formats, targeting options, creative approaches, and campaign settings. By trying out new strategies, you can identify what works best for your target audience and improve campaign performance.

c) Optimize Budget Allocation: Based on the performance data and ROI analysis, adjust your budget allocation to focus on the campaigns or ad sets that deliver the highest return. This helps optimize your advertising spend and maximize the impact of your budget.

d) Incorporate User Feedback: Pay attention to user feedback, comments, and engagement metrics on your TikTok ads. User feedback can provide valuable insights into how your ads are being received and can guide you in making improvements to resonate better with your audience.

e) Stay Updated on TikTok Trends and Features: Keep yourself informed about the latest trends, features, and updates on the TikTok platform. TikTok regularly introduces new advertising options and tools that can enhance your campaigns. By staying up to date, you can leverage these advancements to improve your ad strategy.

f) Seek Expert Guidance: Consider consulting with advertising professionals, agencies, or experts who specialize in TikTok advertising. They can provide valuable insights, strategies, and recommendations to optimize your campaigns based on their experience and expertise.

By continuously evaluating your performance, making data-driven decisions, and refining your advertising strategy, you can enhance the effectiveness and ROI of your TikTok ad campaigns over time.

Remember, the digital advertising landscape is dynamic, and what works today may not work tomorrow. Therefore, it's crucial to stay agile, adapt to changes, and continuously iterate and refine your approach to keep your TikTok ad campaigns successful.

Chapter 10: Case Studies and Success Stories

In this chapter, we will explore real-life case studies and success stories of brands and businesses that have achieved notable results through TikTok ad campaigns. By studying these examples, you can gain insights into effective strategies and learn valuable lessons from industry experts. Let's dive into some inspiring case studies.

10.1 Case Study: Brand X - Driving Brand Awareness with TikTok Ads

Brand X, a fashion retailer targeting Gen Z consumers, wanted to increase brand awareness and engagement among their target audience. They launched a TikTok ad campaign utilizing the platform's immersive and engaging ad formats. Here's what they did:

a) Captivating Storytelling: Brand X created a series of visually appealing and creative TikTok ads that showcased their latest fashion collections. They leveraged TikTok's short-form video format to tell compelling stories and capture the attention of their audience.

b) Collaboration with TikTok Creators: To enhance the authenticity and reach of their campaign, Brand X collaborated with popular TikTok creators who aligned with their brand values and target audience. These creators featured Brand X products in their videos, amplifying the reach and engagement of the campaign.

c) Trend Integration: Brand X kept a pulse on the latest TikTok trends and challenges and incorporated them into their ad campaign. By joining relevant trends, they capitalized on the platform's viral nature and increased their ad's visibility and shareability.

The results of Brand X's TikTok ad campaign were impressive. They experienced a significant increase in brand awareness, with their ads reaching millions of users and generating high engagement rates. The campaign also led to a boost in website traffic and conversions, contributing to the brand's overall growth.

10.2 Case Study: Company Y - Driving Sales through Influencer Collaborations

Company Y, an e-commerce business specializing in beauty and skincare products, aimed to drive sales and conversions through TikTok ads. They adopted a strategy centered on influencer collaborations. Here's how they achieved success:

a) Influencer Selection: Company Y identified TikTok influencers with a significant following and engaged audience within their target market. They carefully vetted influencers for alignment with their brand values and authenticity.

b) Product Showcasing: The chosen influencers created engaging content showcasing Company Y's products in a natural and relatable manner. They demonstrated product usage, shared reviews, and offered exclusive discount codes to their followers.

c) Call-to-Action and Tracking: Each influencer's content included a clear call-to-action, encouraging viewers to visit the Company Y website or use the provided discount code. Company Y utilized UTM parameters and the TikTok Pixel to track conversions and attribute them to specific influencer campaigns.

The collaboration with TikTok influencers resulted in a substantial increase in sales for Company Y. The influencer-generated content garnered high engagement and drove traffic to their website, leading to a significant boost in conversions. The trust and influence of the chosen influencers played a crucial role in establishing credibility and encouraging their followers to make purchases.

10.3 Insights from Industry Experts

Alongside real-life case studies, it's valuable to gain insights and strategies from industry experts who have extensive experience in TikTok advertising. Here are some key takeaways:

a) Authenticity is Key: TikTok is a platform known for its authentic and unfiltered content. To succeed with TikTok ads, it's essential to maintain an authentic and genuine tone. Users respond positively to ads that feel native to the platform and align with their interests.

b) Embrace Creativity and Storytelling: TikTok offers a creative playground for advertisers. Leveraging the platform's unique ad formats and storytelling capabilities can capture users' attention and create memorable experiences. Experiment with different creative approaches and formats to stand out and engage your audience.

c) Stay Agile and Experiment: TikTok is a rapidly evolving platform with ever-changing trends and user preferences. To stay ahead, be open to experimentation and adapt your strategies accordingly. Test different ad formats, targeting options, and messaging to discover what resonates best with your target audience.

d) Leverage Influencer Partnerships: Influencer marketing can be a powerful tool on TikTok. Collaborating with TikTok influencers who align with your brand values and have a strong following can help amplify your message and increase engagement. Choose influencers whose audience closely matches your target demographic for maximum impact.

e) Monitor and Optimize Performance: Continuously monitor the performance of your TikTok ad campaigns. Analyze metrics such as engagement rates, conversion rates, and ROI to identify areas for improvement. Make data-driven decisions and optimize your campaigns based on the insights gained.

f) Stay Updated on Platform Features: TikTok frequently introduces new features, ad formats, and targeting options. Stay informed about these updates and explore how you can leverage them to enhance your campaigns. Being up to date with the latest trends and tools can give you a competitive edge.

g) Audience-Centric Approach: Understand your target audience deeply. Analyze their preferences, behaviors, and content consumption patterns on TikTok. Tailor your ad campaigns to resonate with their interests and create a personalized experience. The more you understand and cater to your audience, the more successful your TikTok ads will be.

Learning from successful case studies and industry experts can provide valuable insights and inspiration for your TikTok ad campaigns. Apply these lessons to your own strategies, while also being open to experimentation and adaptation to find the approaches that work best for your brand and audience.

Remember, TikTok is a dynamic platform that requires continuous adaptation and optimization. Stay up to date with the latest trends, features, and best practices to stay ahead of the curve. Embrace creativity, experiment, and leverage the power of TikTok's community to create impactful ad campaigns.

Chapter 11: The Future of TikTok Advertising

As TikTok continues to grow in popularity and evolve as a social media platform, the future of TikTok advertising holds exciting opportunities for businesses. In this chapter, we will explore some predictions, trends, and emerging features that can shape the future of TikTok ads. Additionally, we will discuss how to stay ahead of the competition in this dynamic landscape.

11.1 Predictions and Trends for TikTok Ads

a) Increased Advertising Options: As TikTok expands its advertising capabilities, we can expect to see new and innovative ad formats being introduced. This could include interactive ads, augmented reality (AR) experiences, and more immersive storytelling formats that captivate users' attention and drive engagement.

b) Enhanced Targeting Capabilities: TikTok is likely to refine and expand its targeting options, allowing advertisers to reach even more specific audience segments. This could include advanced demographic targeting, interest-based targeting, and contextual targeting based on video content. Improved targeting capabilities will enable advertisers to deliver more relevant and personalized ads to their desired audiences.

c) Integration of E-commerce Features: TikTok has already started experimenting with e-commerce features, allowing users to shop directly within the app. In the future, we can expect more seamless integration of e-commerce functionalities into TikTok ads, enabling businesses to drive sales and conversions directly from their ad campaigns.

d) Continued Rise of Influencer Marketing: Influencer marketing is a powerful strategy on TikTok, and it is expected to continue growing. As the platform evolves, we may see more sophisticated influencer collaboration options, such as long-term partnerships, brand ambassadorships, and influencer-led content series. Brands that leverage influencer marketing effectively can tap into the influencer's engaged audience and benefit from their credibility and authenticity.

11.2 Emerging Features and Opportunities

a) TikTok Ad Network: TikTok is exploring the creation of an ad network that extends beyond the TikTok app itself. This could potentially allow advertisers to reach TikTok's vast user base through partner apps and websites, expanding the reach and impact of TikTok ad campaigns.

b) Shoppable Livestreams: TikTok's live streaming feature has gained popularity, and there is an opportunity to integrate shoppable features into these live streams. This would enable businesses to showcase products or services in real-time and provide users with the ability to make purchases directly within the live stream.

c) Personalization and Customization: TikTok is likely to focus on further enhancing the personalization and customization options for advertisers. This could include more dynamic ad templates, personalized product recommendations, and tailored ad experiences based on user preferences and behavior.

11.3 Staying Ahead of the Competition

a) Embrace Early Adoption: To stay ahead of the competition, be proactive in adopting new features and ad formats as they become available on TikTok. Early adopters have the advantage of exploring new opportunities and capturing the attention of users who are eager for fresh content.

b) Continuous Learning and Optimization: Keep abreast of the latest trends, best practices, and changes in the TikTok advertising landscape. Continuously analyze and optimize your ad campaigns based on data and insights to ensure maximum performance and effectiveness.

c) Creativity and Authenticity: TikTok is a platform that celebrates creativity and authenticity. Stand out from the competition by creating unique, engaging, and authentic content that resonates with your target audience. Encourage user-generated content and foster a sense of community around your brand.

d) Collaboration with TikTok Influencers: Influencer collaborations can provide a competitive edge. Identify relevant TikTok influencers who align with your brand and develop partnerships that drive engagement and amplify your message. Leverage the creativity and influence of these creators to expand your reach and build trust with your target audience.

e) Test and Experiment: The landscape of TikTok advertising is constantly evolving, so it's essential to embrace a culture of testing and experimentation. Try different ad formats, messaging variations, targeting options, and creative approaches to discover what resonates best with your audience. Continuously monitor the performance of your campaigns and optimize them based on the data and insights you gather.

f) Data-Driven Decision Making: Make data-driven decisions by closely analyzing the performance metrics of your TikTok ad campaigns. Utilize the analytics provided by TikTok Ads Manager to gain insights into user behavior, engagement rates, and conversion metrics. Use this data to identify trends, patterns, and areas for improvement, allowing you to refine your strategies and stay ahead of the competition.

g) Cross-Platform Promotion: TikTok doesn't exist in isolation. Consider integrating your TikTok ad campaigns with other marketing channels to create a cohesive and comprehensive brand presence.

Cross-promote your TikTok content on other social media platforms, your website, or through email marketing to maximize exposure and reach a wider audience.

h) Stay Agile and Adapt: TikTok is a platform known for its rapid evolution and user-driven trends. Stay agile and adapt your strategies to align with the changing dynamics of the platform. Keep a close eye on emerging features, trends, and user preferences to ensure your TikTok ad campaigns remain fresh, relevant, and engaging.

Conclusion

Throughout this ebook, we have explored the world of TikTok ads and uncovered strategies, tips, and best practices to help you harness the power of this dynamic platform for your marketing campaigns. Let's recap the key learnings and takeaways from our journey:

1. TikTok's Potential: TikTok has emerged as a dominant force in the social media landscape, offering immense opportunities for businesses to connect with their target audience in unique and engaging ways. Its user base, creative features, and viral nature make it an ideal platform for brand promotion.

2. Crafting Compelling Ads: Creating attention-grabbing TikTok ads requires a deep understanding of the platform's ad formats, storytelling techniques, and trends. By leveraging creativity, authenticity, and staying on top of the latest trends, you can create ads that resonate with your audience and drive engagement.

3. Targeting and Optimization: Effective targeting and optimization are crucial for success on TikTok. By defining your target audience, utilizing TikTok's

targeting options, monitoring campaign performance, and implementing optimization strategies, you can ensure your ads reach the right people at the right time.

4. Influencer Marketing: Collaborating with TikTok influencers can significantly amplify the reach and impact of your ad campaigns. Choosing the right influencers, building partnerships, and leveraging their influence can help you tap into their engaged audience and establish a strong brand presence on TikTok.

5. Challenges and Pitfalls: Ad fatigue, algorithm changes, and negative feedback are common challenges you may face on TikTok. By adopting proactive strategies to combat these challenges, such as refreshing your content, staying updated with platform changes, and effectively managing feedback, you can navigate these obstacles and maintain a positive brand image.

6. Ethical Considerations: Adhering to TikTok's advertising policies, complying with local regulations, and prioritizing user privacy and data security are essential for maintaining trust with your audience and avoiding legal issues.

7. Measuring Success: Key performance indicators (KPIs), conversion tracking, and ROI evaluation are vital for measuring the effectiveness of your TikTok ad campaigns. By analyzing data, optimizing campaigns, and iterating your strategies, you can continuously improve your results and maximize your return on investment.

As you conclude this ebook, I encourage you to implement the strategies and techniques outlined here and adapt them to the ever-evolving landscape of TikTok advertising. Embrace the dynamic nature of the platform, stay updated with new features and trends, and continue to refine and optimize your campaigns.

TikTok offers a world of possibilities for businesses of all sizes and industries. By leveraging its creative tools, engaging with the TikTok community, and staying ahead of the competition, you can unlock new opportunities, expand your reach, and drive meaningful results for your brand.

Now it's time to take action. Dive into the world of TikTok ads, experiment with different approaches, and let your creativity shine. Embrace the power of TikTok advertising and position your brand for success in this exciting and rapidly evolving landscape.

Wishing you the best of luck on your TikTok advertising journey!

Appendix

Glossary of Important Terms and Acronyms:

1. TikTok: A popular social media platform that allows users to create and share short videos.

2. TikTok Ads: Advertising features and tools offered by TikTok to promote businesses and brands on the platform.

3. TikTok Ads Manager: The platform's advertising management tool that enables advertisers to create, manage, and optimize their TikTok ad campaigns.

4. Ad Fatigue: A phenomenon where users become less responsive to an ad due to repeated exposure.

5. Banner Blindness: The tendency of users to ignore or overlook banner ads, typically due to their familiarity or placement on a webpage.

6. KPIs: Key Performance Indicators, which are metrics used to measure the performance and success of an advertising campaign.

7. CTR: Click-Through Rate, the ratio of users who click on an ad to the total number of users who view it.

8. ROI: Return on Investment, a measure of the profitability of an investment relative to its cost.

9. A/B Testing: A method of comparing two different versions of an ad or campaign to determine which one performs better.

10. Pixel: A piece of code placed on a website to track user activity and gather data for ad targeting and retargeting purposes.

Additional Resources and References:

1. TikTok for Business (https://www.tiktok.com/business): The official website of TikTok's business platform, offering insights, case studies, and advertising resources.

2. TikTok Ads Help Center (https://ads.tiktok.com/help): A comprehensive resource center provided by TikTok, offering guides, tutorials, and FAQs on advertising on the platform.

3. TikTok Marketing Partner Program (https://www.tiktok.com/business/en-US/partner-program): A program that connects businesses with trusted TikTok marketing partners who can provide expertise and support in TikTok advertising.

4. Social Media Today (https://www.socialmediatoday.com): A website providing news, insights, and resources on social media marketing, including TikTok advertising.

5. "TikTok Ads: The Ultimate Guide" by Social Media Examiner (https://www.socialmediaexaminer.com/tiktok-ads-the-ultimate-guide): An in-depth guide that covers various aspects of TikTok advertising, including campaign setup, ad formats, targeting, and optimization.

6. "TikTok Advertising: The Ultimate Guide for Beginners" by Hootsuite (https://blog.hootsuite.com/tiktok-advertising): A beginner's guide to TikTok advertising, covering the basics, ad formats, targeting options, and best practices.

These resources provide valuable information, tips, and insights to further enhance your understanding of TikTok advertising and support your journey towards successful campaigns.

TikTok Banner: Designed by myriammira / Freepik

Note: As the TikTok platform evolves, new resources and references may become available. It is recommended to stay updated with the latest information and resources provided by TikTok and reputable marketing sources to ensure you have the most relevant and accurate information for your advertising efforts.